The Dead
Are So
Disappointing

The Dead
Are So
Disappointing

Poems by Katherine Fishburn

Michigan State University Press
East Lansing

∞ The paper used in this publication meets the minimum requirements
of ANSI/NISO Z39.48-1992 (R 1997) (Permanence of Paper).

Michigan State University Press
East Lansing, Michigan 48823-5202

Printed and bound in the United States of America.

04 03 02 01 00   1 2 3 4 5

Library of Congress Cataloging-in-Publication Data

Fishburn, Katherine, 1944-
  The dead are so disappointing : poems / by Katherine Fishburn.
    p. cm.

  ISBN 0-87013-532-5 (alk. paper)
  1. Fathers and daughters—Poetry. 2. Death—Poetry. I. Title.
PS3556.I7913 D43 1999
811'.54—dc21

                                                    99-6505
                                                    CIP

Book and Cover Design by Michael J. Brooks

Visit Michigan State University Press on the World Wide Web
        www.msu.edu/unit/msupress

the year shuts down
too soon it's night
too long

Contents

Fish Story 1

The Faster I Run 2

Rigidity Becomes You .3

Mothers and Fathers 5

Entirely at Me 6

A Son Herself 8

The Professor's Daughter 10

Keep the Drama 12

I Cannot Yet Tell 13

A Phantom of the Day 15

A Minor Pleasure 16

The Dead Are So Disappointing 19

Until I Arrive 21

But Flesh 24

When I Die 26

If Breasts Are Weapons 29

The Pain from My Throat 31

Freud Taught Us to Think 34

Terror of Heights 39

The Grids of the Periodic Table 42

Habeas Corpus 45

Mine for the Taking .49

As Much as His Own .54

Tasting the Wind 58

The Censor and the Checkbook 62

Fish Story

The last time I fished with my father
the sky was bronze with the weather
and the road translucent with unfallen rain
. . . for the earth had tipped over.

We tended the river, my father and I,
while he watched the line he had cast
I looked for life in the shallows
. . . you eyed my fatal collection of flies.

Calling me to his side as he stood on the bank,
he showed me a carp heavy and dark
locked in the wavering shadows of roots
. . . sucking the life from the rich foreign water.

When later I stumbled and fell in that water
. . . I fished you out: my catch of the day
the limbs of my translated daughter
festooned with ribbons of minnows and rush.

In recasting these lines to give my life form
I often have trouble defining just what
I've been thrown and what is my own

But this much I know: of that close summer day
when the reel stopped its turning I remember the living
. . . but never the drowning.

The Faster I Run

some days when I look in the mirror
everyone's there—
and I can't find myself for the crowd

there are so many ways
I have tried to be different:
tried to avoid the sins of my father
tried to avoid the faults of my mother
but I cannot escape them

and the faster I run, the sooner we meet
in a smashing collision
that sends the parts of me I thought were my own
into a thousand spinning directions

that, when they reverse and return,
show themselves not to be me
but motherfathersisteretalia

and the moment of reunification
is so sudden and thorough
I implode with the knowledge
of kismet—

who then has written this poem?

Rigidity Becomes You

you don't want to do that, he said
but I did
whatever it was—I no longer remember
only the pattern remains

his way of keeping me within the lines

❧

as an adult I heard it repeated on at least two occasions:
telling my husband and me
that we didn't want to take the route
we had mapped out for our trip
for he had a better way he would show us
if we'd pay close attention

❧

the next time it was my sister
telling her two year old
you don't want to do that
as he struggled to climb on the gym
instead of the swing she had sanctioned

taking his side, I called her on it
said: you sound just like dad
what do you mean, she replied

you don't want to do that, I said
what you mean is you don't want him to do it

that's what dad always said
you don't want to do it
but clearly he does
or he wouldn't be trying

well, she retorted, caught out,
her cheeks red with the cold and the thought
why shouldn't I sound like him
I'm his daughter

do I sound like him too?
keeping small children off gyms
and strictly between the lines
I have drawn
from my own designs—

but executed in the voice of my father
more mine than I like to admit
at least to his daughter

Mothers and Fathers

who is to say which had the greater power,
mother or father

for years it seemed to me
that the advantage lay with my father,
who could turn a dinner party
into an occasion of public humiliation
with a flick of his tongue

while my mother took the abuse without speaking,
merely allowing the tears to gather
but never spill over

though I tried to defend her as best I knew how
and shouted harsh truths to my father,
my mother already had her champion
and I was instructed to beg his forgiveness

it was a moment of personal achievement
when in my late forties
I switched loyalties and defended myself to my father

but I have yet to confront my mother
whose tears continue
to make me protective

she tells me I frighten her
but my words are no match for her weeping

Entirely at Me

how to reconcile
the funny, affable man
of public repute
with the man I knew at home?

the man who never left others
feeling inferior
in their own intellectuality
when I never felt anything else?

when my father died
the journey home involved
multiple dimensions—the past
drawing me in like a spent trout
at the end of a line on a long afternoon

for years I had fought off those memories
of trying to be smarter
more clever
faster to get the point of a joke
or follow a proof

I had forgotten the bitter
unrecognized competition between my sister
and me to be thought second-best
in the rankings, first seed always already
claimed by my father

I had forgotten, if not overcome,
the fear that made my stomach lurch
like an automobile with a worn-out suspension

the fear that kept me silent and cautious
until it would erupt unexpectedly into anger
at the worst possible moment

how could I have so thoroughly forgotten
the look of serene satisfaction on my sister's face
as she cut her eyes in my direction,
secure in the knowledge
that, one more time,
our father's wrath
would now be directed
entirely
at me

A Son Herself

my father's parting gift
which my mother dutifully passed on
was to announce
that he always wished
he had had a son

to which my sister and I
both responded,
as though in unison—
I thought *I* was the son

as first-born
I took his profession
(with a twist)
each book offered as evidence
I was worthy

I tried very hard to be good
but the voice that sits in judgment
is that of my father
and has yet to be pleased

a friend of my father's
informs us
that the only time he ever heard
my father brag
was when he spoke of his grandson

not being a son herself
my sister
recognizing the value
instead
produced one

The Professor's Daughter

in truth there was a lot to mourn
in the passing of this man,
my father
it isn't only orphans
who would envy me his parenting
but in the testimonials
others have brought forward
I hear a man I did not know

how can it be that he taught
another how to be a good father
to his sons
when I felt his neglect so soon?

why didn't it last, that which had begun
so well? I think I was four when I fell in the river
and when I saw the nest of baby snakes I cannot recall—
I also fell from the bleachers at a very young age,
falling apparently being what I did with my father;
I must have been about twelve or thirteen
when he bought me an outfielder's glove
and taught me to bat right and left handed;
when I missed the unit on signed numbers
he brought me up to speed;
the last thing I remember he taught me
was how to drive like a man—and I do

but where, in these memories, are conversations,
moments he asks what I'm thinking or feeling?

I guess one shouldn't expect
a teacher to act like a father
but I've often wished
he could have made just one more exception
at least for his daughter

Keep the Drama

in the months since my father died
my mother has averred more than once
that there's a play in all of this
if only someone could write it

I know what she means
and envision one written by an amalgam
of O'Neill and Tennessee Williams
but I'm no playwright, only a poet
so the dramatic action will be reduced accordingly:

that my parents loved me there is no doubt—
they fed me, dressed me, and housed me
they taught me, led me, chastened me

but when it came time to have my own family
I chose not to have children,
only husbands and dogs—with an orphan cat
to complete the album

having watched one child suffer
I knew I couldn't watch two

and by the time I learned that stories could change,
that old scripts didn't have to be followed
it was too late to assemble the characters
for another production

but we do just fine, thank you,
and keep the drama
to a bare minimum

I Cannot Yet Tell

I cannot yet tell
which was worse:

to engage my father's unspeaking gaze
converged on infinity
as he shuffled half-naked
beyond the concept of shame,
out of the bathroom
into the room that he shared
with a man who couldn't stop talking
(but who, the director assured us,
came from a very fine family)

or to see my mother
in a single, hopeless
but pitying gesture

remove from his head the frivolous party hat,
made of stiff blue and green foil
in a holiday pattern,
that had been held firmly in place
by an elasticized band
in sure anticipation
of a violent, joy-filled moment
that had not occurred

the elastic restraint
one of many he endured
at the end
brought under his ill-shaved chin,

13

like the others,
by an aide too callow
to imagine
what it might be like
to regard the passing of the year
as of absolutely
no consequence
at all

A Phantom of the Day

can a daughter ever
gaze upon her father's nakedness
without consequence?

old, shorn of speech
and the freedom to refuse
but still capable of working
the bindings loose
and walking the polished halls
in sad confusion
eyes cloudy with cataracts
and an inborn knowledge
of what lay only days away

of all the appetites only those
for anger and sweets remained
so I fed him candied fruit
rolled in sugar, bit by bit
left him chocolate by the bed

was it me his gaze took leave of
as I walked away?
or was I, too,
another phantom
of the day?

A Minor Pleasure

as elder daughter
it fell to me
to organize the dying
and the dead

given no choice
and even less time,
with the aid not of divine
but expert, highly paid intervention,
I transformed two old people,
care-giver and cared-for,
into the arcane language of assets and trusts
which I hoped would serve to protect them

shortly thereafter, too driven
to recognize the exhaustion depleting myself
I bristled, on cue, with the fixed admonition
that gave my mother,
spent from managing two lives
and a habit of self-sacrificing,
the permission she craved
to tap into her own vast reserves
of still resolution
and leave my father,
a brilliant man
by all accounting,
among the senile and insane

❧

would we agree, the documents queried,
to mild restraints for his own protection?
we would, we wrote, with a sigh of relief
having gratefully transferred the obligation—
momentarily having forgotten,
in our hunger for sleep,
just who it was we had committed
to spend his final days
in an alien place
peopled only
by strangers

&

yet to our astonishment
we shortly found
he didn't seem to mind
that we had left him there,
only that it took so long
each time
to solve the puzzle
of the safety catch
designed
for those of less
perseverance

&

I comfort myself as I can
these days
so find a minor pleasure
in the fact
that every day the staff submitted
(as the law required they must)
a dry report that read:

this patient
yet again
has unlocked the secret
of his universe and
fallen
on
his head

The Dead Are So Disappointing

the dead are so disappointing
leaving us here
in the present
to work out on our own
the problem of anger and dread
we feel at their passing

though some have convinced themselves
(or so they aver)
that dying is life's last great adventure
to be embraced like scaling a mountain,
cresting the rapids,
or mapping a wilderness
I personally
given the chance
would gladly pass on
the experience

no, he was not afraid
he answered when asked
in a rare moment
of personal confession
no point to it really
since he wouldn't be there
if you considered it

but, as it turned out,
it wasn't exactly a light switch
as he completed the circuit
but more like a rheostat,

as daily there was less of him
and more of the corpse we carry within;
for days the man he had been
resisted the inert body he would become
till finally the blue of necrosis
signaled the battle was done
and with one barely detectable
exhalation he gave himself up
to the unknown

yet he gave me no help
this man who always knew everything
in preparing myself
for my own
fleshy extinction—
for if,
as he claimed,
there was nothing to fear
why, then, did he fight
so hard
at the end?

Until I Arrive

masquerading as the infinite hope
of the future's unmet contingencies,
the past extends out before us
like an alluvial fan down an incline
on the outer slopes
of an extinct volcano, spent with too much expression
and gone cold with the snowfall—
or the seedpod of an angiosperm
bursting forth in the spring
with its fate sealed within

all my life without even knowing it
I have carried inside me
the weight of another's thwarted expectations
mapping my journey to ease the burden
of disappointments unceasing,
convinced that the ache I could never put down
was born of my own search for perfection

what did he long for, my father,
when he learned the title soon would be his?
did he have the imagination
at the time
to wish for a son—
or did that only come later
with the birth of my sister
and my own maturation?

he never said much to me
except for giving instruction
in physics and math
and behavioral matters,
such as the virtue of rectitude
or the lesson hard-won that being late for dinner
was never an option—
or, on occasion, correcting my childish pronunciation,
he finding it wrong,
it going unspoken
that his word was not to be questioned

his taciturnity having expanded
into legendary proportions of silence
within our four-person household
of native speakers of English,
I never gave a great deal of thought
as to why, except for the training in various disciplines,
our verbal exchanges went through my mother

she who always assured me
of his love and his pride in his offspring

having been warned not to tell him
what I had done, or been thinking
it came as a shock, when one evening
as I talked with my mother of my style of teaching,
he glanced up from the paper that he had been reading,

looked over his half glasses,
and proclaimed in a fiat—
typical of what passed in his eyes
for a complete conversation between father and child,
a comment so fleeting I might have missed it
had I not been accustomed to heeding his precepts—
that I, I who had seemed to exist only in faulty translation,
I who was closer to fifty than forty
I was, indeed, in his estimation, a formidable woman
and shouldn't be shocked by my students' reaction

I treasure that judgment
from a man who made his living
evaluating others' intelligence
(that being one of the things
we professors get paid for)

I learned later, however,
that each word had been carefully chosen,
as one might have expected
from a man who valued precision
since, after all my accomplishments,
he still at the end wished for a son

what past lurks around the next corner,
I wonder,
biding its time
until I arrive?

But Flesh

I excel at imagining death
not the act
the end

I envision the objects
I own
that will outlast me
and sometimes resent
their brute durability
yet I persist in acquiring them

not believing in god
or the hereafter,
and having no offspring,
I wonder:
are these many possessions
my genes' confused bid
to insure immortality in cultural dispersion?

I see my gardens
grown wild and unkempt
neglected yet flourishing
unchecked by my governing hand

itself gone rotten and eaten
by worms and bacteria
who have no taste for dirt or fruit
but flesh

chilled discordant flesh
the sweetmeat of death

flesh I envision
gone soft with decay

&

can flesh imagine
me gone?

the great virtuoso
who yet cannot lift a finger
or sing a stanza
in aid of digestion

or think her way through
the vena cava
or heal a wound
or fight an infection

&

dear flesh
without whom nothing
bright flesh
whose knowledge
I own

but cannot make speak
except to imagine
it gone

When I Die

Nine books in five years—
can it be?
And all after eighty.
It's beyond comprehension
but got him a headline.

When I die, on the other hand,
it will go largely unremarked.
No national obituaries for me.

I assert this not out of regret or self-pity—
for I learned young
to find comfort
in green moments of solitude,
thrusting my hands
into the companionable dirt of my garden,
giving astilbe and hosta the shade that they need,
reordering the world in my writing

and always,
always
gazing into the tranquil eyes pooled at my feet,
as clear and brown as a pond in spring,
which have done better than most
in reflecting the world back to me.

Poor things, being dogs
they had no choice but to love me
but took some comfort, I'm sure,
in the certain knowledge
that I had brought them into the pack
and carefully explained just where they fit in.
It does not overstate it to claim
that my favorite people are animals—
or to think
except for my husband
and a handful of friends
they above all will know that I've gone.

The skilled craftsmen,
the painters and plumbers
whose work
I've admired and praised, often in writing,
might wonder why the house calls they make
have a little more routine conversation,
but I doubt they'll remember my name.
The doctors might long for another patient
as silly and irreverent as I
who took their advice as pragmatic solutions
and never as gospel—
but I feel pretty certain
that most of their nurses won't.

Of my students, who must number now
in the thousands, some will write letters
of praise and thanksgiving,
some no doubt
(as I learned with my father)
will wish they had sent them
before I had died.
While others will feel smug they've outlasted me,
youth being the single advantage
they had in the classroom.

Those who have found value
in the ideas I gave voice to
will regret that not all of them
found their way into print—
so they will need to be reminded
of the maxim
by which I structured my thinking
that there are only six ideas
in the first place
and not to be
overly impressed with my skill in deploying them.

If Breasts Are Weapons

If breasts are weapons
(as some claim them to be),
mine have armed only the opposition.
The first time I knew their potential for harm
I was nine and, having nothing to hide,
had gone into town with no shirt on.
As soon as I arrived, I knew the extent
of my naive miscalculation.
What had gone unnoticed at home
became in the square a blazing signification
of my fated potential for womanhood.
All I recall of the trip that day is my shame
as I suddenly knew,
with a shudder of realization
that will not go away,
I had lost the unspoken privilege
to be seen naked without embarrassment.
No physical change marked my ascension
out of the genus of childhood,
yet none was needed. In my thoughts I had already
become a woman.

The passing of childhood was much later affirmed
by my mother's stern admonition
that I had grown too old—if not too mammalian—
to suffer unclothed my father's attention.
Too soon they arrived, these unwelcome breasts,
though they were late by my friends' computation
and far too small to be satisfactory, even to me.

Yet they were sufficient to work the change
in my father. No longer could we pretend
that he had had a son, after all.
Lost were the days of fishing and baseball.

Yet the only change I experienced was the unwelcome
sensation of shame.

Like fear, my shame grew
where my breasts did not
and emitted a scent all its own, distinctive and fatal,
which my classmates, drawn into an ancient alliance,
sniffed out with a feral efficiency,
gauging with instinctive clarity how best to effect the kill.
Needing a weapon to counter
what they regarded as my unseemly foreign intelligence,
they turned the size of my breasts to their striking advantage,
inhaling with drunken delight
the overpowering smell of mortification,
as I clasped my blameless breasts to myself
in an embrace meant not to protect
but to smother them.

The Pain from My Throat

I love the look
of pleased anticipation
with which my dogs
engage my idle attention,
utterly guileless in its gift of reflection
folding myself into their doggy perception

it is a look so pure
and unprotected
that it can be matched only
by the open faces of the harmlessly insane
or, by a new lover still secure
in the self-affirming certitude
his adoring gaze
will be returned

—or, by a child too young
to have learned
the art of stoic deception

I had been to the doctor that day
for radium treatments:

long copper rods
with the taste
of uncomprehending
fear

and the smell of smiling, unyielding
medical assurance
had been thrust down my throat
by way of my nasal passage

gagging reflexively
I tried to discharge
the sanctioned invaders,
but the expert hand guiding the rods
overcame my attempts
at repulsion
and burned out a bit
of my body
as planned

when my father the chemist
came home that evening
I raised my eyes in childish certainty
that he, at least, would see,
as my mother had not,
that the day's
routine procedure
required adult intervention
and should never have been done
on his very own
exceptional
daughter

intercepting the mute plea I was making
before it was finished,
he informed me in the voice
that drove the pain from my throat
into my belly, where it was no stranger
that he was ashamed
of me
for being

a bad
girl

Freud Taught Us to Think

Freud taught us to think
that for daughters
the fault lay with our mothers
the distinction between us
being crudely achieved—
an argument embraced by a battalion
of otherwise skeptical women
for nearly a decade
who, armed with new-found ambitions,
lay their faults without shame
at their mother's immaculate doorsteps,
demanding domestic redress
if not reparation

but I'm here to tell you they're wrong
Freud and his women
the fault lay with our fathers
for now that mine's gone
I cannot move on

I had actually hoped years ago
when first I imagined his dying
that it might liberate me
from the scornful voice
that corrects all my failings

but coincident with his leaving
I have developed a new imperfection
the worse so far I have known,
one unlike the others
I am helpless
to amend or surmount on my own

this defect is prolonging my grieving
driving it deep into my muscles
where it keeps me awake at night

for in the same year I lost both
my father
and my hair—a grammatical construction
that would be amusing
or even a zeugma if the pain
were not
indistinguishable

of the two losing my hair was the harder
and most unexpected,
catching me completely off guard—
for I once had welcomed the prospects of aging
as far as my hair went,
seeing my mother's convert into bullion

I wrote my father's obituary
and delivered a eulogy
what have I done for my hair?

though most of my friends had never met him
(living out of town as he did
and not being reliably charming)
many sent cards to acknowledge his passing
but who makes sympathy cards for hair loss
and whoever would send them?

since I am clever at concealing it
and my husband assures me that no one can tell,
who even knows that a part of me has gone missing?

yet what I have lost has eaten into the core of my being
like a demon I love too well to let go

I cannot recount
what bargains I have struck with fate
or those I would still make
if only my hair would grow back

if I live to the conventional age
for old ladies today
I will have spent exactly one third of my life
with neither a father
nor a full head of hair

now who can ask sympathy for such a comparison,
to whom do I turn for true
understanding?

the expert I consulted
coolly informed me,
with grammatical inexactitude but speaking ex cathedra,
from the airless heights
of his famed professional station—
when I confessed how hard it was
to deal with my loss
and could he give me assurance it wouldn't get worse—
that it was hard for everyone
(presumably including himself,
though this went unmentioned,
he being the doctor and I but the patient)
to find they are losing their hair

why didn't that comfort me?

my hairdresser said in shocked disapproval
when I reported the story to her
that he should have known better
that highly paid doctor
didn't he realize that losing my hair
was like losing a part of my body,
an arm or a leg
and mourning was part of the process
of grieving

on another occasion
when I confessed, with embarrassment,
that it hurt worse to lose my hair
than my father,
a young male friend,
as yet with little authority

and even less hair than the doctor,
remarked with a bracing frankness,
and a slight lift of the shoulders for emphasis,
that *his* hair
had always
meant more
to him than his father did

&

for these remarks I am grateful
and will consult with these two again

but though what they offered
far exceeded in insight and informed understanding
the expert's sweeping dismissal
of my plea for human compassion,

their remarks haven't yet helped
the pain
go away

why is it my father I think of
when I look in the mirror everyday?

Terror of Heights

as a child
I always preferred
to pick the grit and dirt myself
out of the wounds I acquired
as easily as other girls amassed
bouquets for their manners and dress

no prom queen
(though later appraisals
would suggest I might have been
had I half tried—or even known how to)
I thought the route
to my daddy's heart
lay in the things he liked to do;
and, above all else, he liked to be entertained,
so I learned, among other embellishments,
to be witty and quick, tell stories—
convulse him with laughter

though my thoughts ran secret and dark
like an underground stream,
with him I was the noisy one on the rock face—
bright, clever narratives bursting out of me
like water crashing downhill
at a pace too swift to be stopped
or traversed

so impressed with the velocity and skill
of my falling down inclines was my family

no one stopped to consider
the moments of black stillness
that curled at my feet,
caught in the rock-laden basins
filling my head
with live water hissing,
trapped water purling and gurgling
dragonflies lit on a reed

photographs that are filed in
a tin hat box
reveal blonde hair
refusing the maternal order of braids
with which I began each day in a torture
of combing and pulling

in the pictures, I appear
untethered, hair flying, mouth open
gaze bold and defiant
belying the role of mommy's
good girl to which I was held
by bridles stronger than plaits

it is only my knees that require
no explanation—
bloody lips, torn open or scabbed over,
the bits of grit from my tumbling
down cliff sides and mountains
carefully picked out and placed on the floor
by my bed
to reduce if not eliminate scarring

❧

though I was loud, I was watchful
and learned young the art
of averting a crisis

what makes a father's anger so total?
so compelling—so final?
why did the streams, the tadpoles
the turtles and mayflies
all coalesce into the mafic peaks
of a rage I found so terrible
to contemplate that I would do anything
to forestall it?

❧

on our hikes in the back country
my husband, who knows anger
but never ascends into the volcanics
of rage,
explains the formation
of mountains—intrusions, subduction
convergence and uplift, his voice
a soothing flow of geologic reason
sinking us both into the chill depths
of deep time
easing my childborn
terror
of heights

The Grids of the Periodic Table

—with thanks to Eugene Linden

the seal grown weary with fighting infection
from the deep tear in its flipper
makes a fatal decision,
half knowing half not,
that it belongs in the sea off Antarctica

gathering what strength it has left
it makes one final dive off the great ice shelf
into the familiar cobalt depths of the water
that has sustained its generation year after year,
trusting to fate to provide fish or companion

when no one arrives to greet its appearance
it thinks for a moment of surfacing
then gives itself over to the prospects of drowning—
releasing the last remnants of air in a sigh no one can hear
and letting go of the idea that had kept it submerged,
the creature politely accepts the gift the ocean has offered

once will has departed
the corpse fulfills the body's intention to rise
but caught in the cold heavy currents
it takes an indirect route
that the living creature would have known to avoid
and soon finds itself
stuck under an ice floe

such a small body, such vast expanses of winter—
the warmth the seal gives to the ocean
no caloric match for the chill that has caught it:
not long after death
ice begins to grow underneath
crystal interlocking with fur
forestalling the rotting of flesh

but gradually over the days
the unmarked tomb laid bare to the sun
(however enfeebled at these far coordinates)
begins itself to decay, releasing its vapors into air
dying for moisture
and slowly, slowly the seal begins its final ascent
its body uncorrupted by its stay in the water gone solid

until finally the seal stands victorious on a pillar of stone
its wound no longer impeding movement
as it gracefully traverses the bay—
stone itself the seal shades the ice column below
ensuring its floating pedestal will never fall into ruin
while in turn the parched arctic gales suck the lifeblood
out of the corpse
keeping it dry for the journey

somewhere in a medical school
my father floats
from room to room
his skeleton preserved from the elements
he once had charted for students—

teaching them the sheer elegance of the move
from one electron to two,
the virtually perfect gradation of halogens
and the nobility of the inert gases
who keep to themselves
and don't mix easily
with baser constituents

such a small body, such vast expanses of winter
both laid out
on the grids of the periodic table

Habeas Corpus

we have the body
except I've never seen one,
though I've heard well-founded rumors
of my father's final translation
from unfinished flesh into corpse:

when he died
my mother had his body shipped off
to the mortuary before I arrived—
where it was taken by the anatomical society
to be skeletonized
so the next generation of medical students
could learn from his frame
what the last one learned from his person

this is no rare event in my life;
in fact it's kind of a pattern—
that a loved one has died
without my verification

the first time it was by design
as the dog who had raised me
virtually unassisted—
the dog I had had to have as a child
or die in my longing, dogs apparently
being part of the gene pool
passed on by my father—

had reached the age
of incontinence and confusion
while I was away getting what all agreed
was a fine education
would I mind, my mother tactfully queried,
if we had Heidi put down?
do it, I said, just don't tell me
I don't want to know

when I came home
after graduation, swelled with my honors degree
and my vision impaired
by the prospects awaiting me in the fall
I did not even see that Heidi was gone

it was ten years before I had another dog
fate taking its time to prepare me—
this one I stole from the neighbors
who had taken her in not out of love
but duty, like accepting the custody
of a foster child one is related to
but doesn't much care for

but me, I fell in love
with this orphaned tri-color beagle
who made her first appearance
unbidden in my open garage
and soon had her in my permanent possession
though to say she owned me in equal measure
is no overstatement

as the years accumulated
month after month
I vowed, in private and public,
when it came time for this dog to depart
I would go with her and hold her next to my heart

though my intentions had been shaped
by mistakes in the past
that I was desperate not to repeat
as it turned out I couldn't fulfill them

at thirteen she was dying of pancreatic failure
but I kept her alive for weeks
out of willful determination,
having to wake her out of profound sleep
when I thought she should eat—
she who had never in her entire lifetime
known what it was to be full—

I knew she was dying
and lay on the floor to ask if she knew what was happening
when she didn't reply
I got out my camera and with the privilege of humans
and the hubris of Avedon
took two photographs of her asleep on the rug,
the modern equivalent
of a death mask
though she wasn't quite gone

against all the evidence
I convinced myself she had enough life
to warrant one more round of medical treatment

so on a Saturday morning marked by parades,
I carted her off to the vet's in my car,
yet she was too weak to stay on the seat
and kept sinking onto the floor—
telling the vet I knew what was happening
I still functioned on the hard edge of denial
and left her there for exploratory surgery
but the x-rays made clear to eyes unclouded by passion
that she was more cancer than beagle
and beyond intervention

though it was late in the weekend
the vet called to tell me
she had expired
and would I want her cremated?
I did—

she had been so stoic with me
I told myself that in leaving her there
I gave her permission to die

only later did it occur to me
that I might want to see her one final time
but the vet's young assistant
having seen more emotion than she knew how to deal with
dissuaded me from coming for Cindy
and in my grief but to my regret
I allowed myself to be convinced—

I buried her ashes in my garden
where she is guarded
by mother of thyme
and a howling wolf
                    on a cliff

Mine for the Taking

to be responsible for death
increases one's gravity,
a perverse sort of growing,
as a centripetal spinning
pulls in the thoughts of the dead

the more I kill the heavier I become
until some days I can hardly move
for all the remains I remember,
the corpses I contain

of all the creatures I have killed
intentionally
and unwittingly
it's the amphibians, turtles,
and crustaceans
that weigh the most in me

when I was seven or eight,
no more than nine
at the outside,
I housed two toads
in a terrarium,
outfitted with moss and plantain,
on top of our new television—
leaf hoppers I fed them in summer,
hamburger on thread the rest of the time;
they liked the meat on a string

having to expend so little effort
at reeling it in
but roasted to death from the dryness
caused by the heat
of the bewitching machine
we couldn't quite bring
ourselves to turn off
in the evening

it was days before I knew they were dead

being a slow learner
when it came to creatures
I brought in from the elements
I let two other souls dry out
when what they needed was freedom

the first was a turtle
that my dog had collected
turtles being a hobby of hers
it spent the summer
in a goldfish bowl,
if not in comfort
at least with plenty of water
but as the days got shorter and darker
it knew for a certainty
that it would need more than gravel
for cover
to get through the winter,
yet repeatedly it set about the hopeless task

of burying itself anew—
it couldn't be reasoned with
so I finally surrendered
and provided a cardboard box
filled with dirt,
for which humble offering
it was gratified well beyond the scope of the gift
and with the conviction of instinct
buried itself alive in trust to the future;

though the garage floor was unheated
and gave the illusion of nature,
no snow breached the walls,
nor could the rain enter
and come spring
the life-giving mantle of dirt
I provided the turtle in autumn
had stolen its moisture,
becoming a carapace without habitation

the other was a crustacean
that seemed almost immortal

with the ruthless need for possession
that marks all children who wander freely,
I had captured a crayfish
during one of the treks
I made on the mountain,
seeking to expand
my collection at the expense of the spring

which appeared to my straightforward creed
that brooked no exceptions
to offer its creatures up for the taking,
so, as was only natural, I took them

the soft-bodied salamander had eluded me,
though not because it was mythic
or dwelled within fire—
more simply, it took to the high ground
and lost itself
in the mysterious channels
of rotting vegetable matter
and the broken pieces of quartz,
milky and moss-grown,
that littered the floor of the forest
from which the pool sprung

the crayfish being less clever
soon had an identity it had not sought out
and as my latest possession
found itself now quite alone
in the depths of my cellar;
though the low altitude
was alien
to this creature native to mountains,
the cool darkness of its new dwelling
bore a consoling resemblance
to what it had known,
and it showed no discontent
in its forced isolation

but I got distracted
by what I can no longer recall
and for days forgot to replenish its water—
once, twice
I resurrected it
by flooding its prison
but these forced hibernations had taken their toll
and by the third time
the crayfish could no longer astound me

I still have dreams
about my amazement
the first time
it crawled out of its rust-colored tomb

but the grief of the third time
has taken root
in my belly,
and sends forth no fruit
but a profusion of foliage—
like a sweet potato planted in soil
too fertile
producing a vine
that entangles itself
in my flesh
with the leaves of the others
whose lives I have taken

though they were never
mine
for the taking

As Much as His Own

I do not think
it is frogs they have in mind
to protect against danger,
when they use the term
attractive nuisance
yet that is what my gardens
have become—
contrary to all my intentions
I keep killing them
when what I have sought to create
is a refuge, a place
where they might flourish among lilies
iris and hyacinth

gardening I learned from my mother
it was my father who taught me
to people my gardens
with spiders and frogs and luminous beetles

for all his domestic tantrums
and impatience with ignorance,
I never knew him to be anything
but courteous to creatures lesser than he
provided, that is, they weren't human beings—
for humans he held
to an exacting standard few could attain
and in the perverse logic he employed near the end
his standards for others grew exponentially

in number and height
as those for himself retreated from sight

≈

I don't think biologists
much *like* nature,
he confessed to me when I was a child
after spotting a particularly resplendent
garden spider, at watch on her web

worried that his otherwise phlegmatic colleague
would be quick to act on the news of her presence
and convert this orbital hunter
into a candidate for his own specimen box—
yet driven by the excitement of detecting her camouflage
designed to quiet the fears of her prey
he himself was compelled,
though he knew better from previous occasions,
to inform everyone he met on his walk
what he had seen by the stream
that followed the road for awhile
before disappearing into the culvert
adorned with masses of jewelweed

≈

as he grew old, he grew ever less cautious
and what he reported gave birth to schemes
of a more serious nature—as I feel quite certain
many of his colleagues dreamed often of pinning *him*

and not spiders or beetles
to the cardboard base of their specimen box;
though CCl_4 had been outlawed by then for commercial
establishments, they would have used it gladly to clean
his clock, stuffing soaked cotton balls into his nostrils
and placidly watching his fury
subside into shock, then the stillness of death

for his smoldering rage with the ill-informed
and poorly spoken
preceded him into all conversations,
like the faint odor of a colostomy bag
needing only the slightest mistake
or mild agitation
to make itself known

how colorful the world must have seemed
in those moments—all flashing purple and red
and deep blue bordered with black,
uneven spikes
of oscillating light
that would rival even nature's displays

you'll kill yourself someday,
my mother would warn him,
indulging yourself in such rage—
you'll have a stroke and then where will I be?
with a husband dead from an apoplectic fit
and me left to offer apologies

❧

she was right about one thing,
my mother, it was a stroke that finally killed him
a massive rupture that left him unconscious
for hours, acquainting him with the silence of death
before it arrived in person to take him, a few short days
after he rallied—
though his last stroke was preceded by a series of small ones
spread out over the years,
stealing bits and pieces of his intelligence,
leaving more space for impatience
and unfounded anger

in the past few months I've wondered often
why, as he cleared all that space in his head
he never invited
the spiders and smooth-skinned amphibians
back in
to weave his thoughts into an orderly pattern
and sing to him
of rapturous love in the standing waters of spring

though he offered no sanctuary at the end
for spiders and frogs,
I do not think it would have displeased him
could he have known
I mourn the frogs' passing
almost
as much as his own

Tasting the Wind

having witnessed first hand
the great brown clouds of swirling dust
pulling up the Great Plains like a black hole pulls in the light
with a ruthless efficiency
wherever they went,
my parents knew the meaning of wind and what it could take
in a day not to mention a decade

they knew
the black earth that had once grown the green shoots of wheat
in place of the tall prairie grasses
that kept the buffalo fat
and nourished the Sioux, needing periodic conflagrations
to keep the blades prolific and sweet

they knew
the vast fields that had kept our soldiers alive
just long enough for them to feed
the maws of the Great War in Europe
that wouldn't be satisfied till it had ten million men in its craw
and twenty million more waiting to die for the cause:

fields of the dead driven into the vaults by the hooves of cattle—
or was it the devil?
carving out a Depression a third the size of Nebraska
from where he could witness the winds and the drought
that ravaged a continent exhausted by combat

when, in our history, has greatness ever coalesced
into such a triumvirate,
when to be Great was to be doomed
or the harbinger of disaster?

though they were too young to remember the fighting
my parents knew only too well how to read the sky
and what the wind threatened
when there was no taste of sweetness to be had on the tongue

there's wind in those clouds
my mother would pronounce from her stoop
at the foot of the Blue Ridge Mountains
where are the children?
girls, come inside
it's beginning to blow
knotting her quaking hands into the homely square of her apron
to keep them from flight—
but twenty years fell away as nothing
while the storm bore down upon us
and forgotten terrors re-emerged in her face
vexed like a hawk by a distraught flock of jackdaws
circling her head

why must you stand with the door open,
she queried my father, risking his anger in her palpable fear,
you know that it's dangerous
you're setting a bad example for the girls

but my father just stood there
as though the wind had taken her words
off in another direction

I knew even then that he heard her
as he leaned his small frame into that of the casing
thrilled with the lightning and thunder
inhaling the ozone that freshened the air
daring the storm to take him,
ready to go if it would

it was he I sided with on these occasions
caught in the drama outdoors
longing for just one more crack of thunder
as the storm threatened the next county over—

I never felt closer to him than when
we flouted my mother's commands
and pulled all the pleasures out of the clouds
that they had to offer before they moved on

much later, my father grew fearful of storms
and would cower in the kitchen
the living room being too full of windows

while my mother, still no lover of storms,
read the clouds as they tore over the mountains
and looked after my father
while she tasted the wind

keeping her own fear well hidden in the folds of her apron
after a lifetime of practice
and making her face a duplicitous mask in order to soothe him
as the lights flickered once, twice
before they went out

it was then that I knew he was dying

The Censor and the Checkbook

don't tell your father,
my mother instructed,
so I kept myself secret, a dutiful child
accepting the rules of the house
I had been born into

but could now fill a book
with the things left unsaid—

if I could only remember
what terrible things I had done
that must be kept from my father

I was too afraid
to do anything really bad—
afraid of my father's staggering anger
afraid of my mother's impending tears

of the two, crying has proved a more lasting threat
as even today I censor myself
if I think what I say will make the tears overflow

but my mother was just part of the zeitgeist,
in her efforts to muzzle her daughter—
these were the fifties, when censorship darkened the skies
with sulfurous thunderheads portending ruin
for those who disclosed themselves too openly

over the airways
Joe McCarthy was tracing in black and white detail
the demented dimensions
of a foreign invasion that impelled all but the bravest
to keep silent about subjects that mattered,
and Hollywood still pre-censored films shown in the theaters—
though they regarded each other with wary combativeness
and Joe won the times they engaged,
these regulators of public morality
had been forced into uneasy collusion
for the good of the country,
lest virtuous citizens choke on the pleasures
of unrestrained congress

while back on the home front, the habit of secrecy
and the domestic pride they had learned from their mothers
kept unhappy wives from sharing with friends
the displaced anger
that was driving them crazy—
so they turned instead to their daughters,
who remained the sole audience for these whispered rebellions
that exhausted themselves in the telling

as for my father, after a lifetime of silence between us,
I found, as he lay dying, that I had very little to say

but this was an occasion that required me to speak
and I knew, at the end, if I hoped to be understood
I would have to speak in his language—

so I gave as my valedictory
a summary recounting of my fiscal
accomplishments—
squatting next to his bed,
I chanted in a low urgent voice
(afraid of being overheard)
the names of the funds and stocks that I owned
and how much they were worth,
topping off the list with an account of how I had balanced
his checkbook, its order gone missing for the past seven months

my father was unimpressed by my financial acumen,
for it had been a year of the bulls
but he seemed grateful to know I had made sense
of the arithmetic mess he had left
as he tumbled slowly into stroke-induced madness
a day at a time
and let it be known, as best he was able,
in a gesture that flooded my heart with what might have been—
that the checkbook had indeed
needed correcting

I wonder now who my mother thought
she was protecting